Goliath *Must* Fall

Goliath
Must
Fall

Winning the Battle Against Your Giants

STUDY GUIDE | SIX SESSIONS

Louie Giglio
with Karen Lee-Thorp

W Publishing Group

An Imprint of Thomas Nelson

Goliath Must Fall Study Guide

Published in Nashville, Tennessee, by W Publishing Group, an imprint of Thomas Nelson. W Publishing Group and Thomas Nelson are registered trademarks of HarperCollins Christian Publishing, Inc.

All Scripture quotations, unless otherwise indicated, are taken from The Holy Bible, New International Version®, NIV®. Copyright © 1973, 1978, 1984, 2011 by Biblica, Inc.™ Used by permission. All rights reserved worldwide.

Scripture quotations marked NKJV are taken from the New King James Version®. © 1982 by Thomas Nelson. Used by permission. All rights reserved.

Thomas Nelson titles may be purchased in bulk for educational, business, fundraising, or sales promotional use. For information, please e-mail SpecialMarkets@ThomasNelson.com.

ISBN 978-0-310-08374-0

First Printing March 2017 / Printed in the United States of America

HB 06.16.2017

Contents

Introduction

Maybe you're familiar with the story of David and Goliath in the Bible. In this epic tale, the nine-foot-tall Goliath holds the entire Israelite army in the grip of fear and humiliation because none of the Israelites dares to go out and fight him. Day after day he taunts them, challenging them to send out one soldier to battle him man to man. Nobody volunteers.

Plenty of us face a similar predicament every day. Although we're not fighting literal giants, our giants are every bit as intimidating and damaging. Maybe it's fear. Maybe it's an addiction. Maybe it's anger. Maybe it's the feeling of rejection, a feeling that permeates so many areas of life. Or maybe it's the sneaky but all-too-familiar giant of comfort that compels us to live for something lesser.

Have you ever felt like King Saul and the Israelite army did? Some kind of giant stands before you, taunting you, harassing you, insulting you. Day after day this giant robs you of your power. You've tried any number of approaches to stop the taunts, but you feel immobilized. Held back. Paralyzed from moving forward in the direction you know you should go. Ultimately, you know you're not living the fullness and freedom of life that God intends for you. If this is part of your story, this study is for you.

This study is all about experiencing the power of Jesus to live in victory over the giant in your life. Each session will equip you with practical, hands-on steps to take after engaging in passages from the Bible and Louie's video talks. In each gathering, expect an opening question, a short Bible study, and then some time taking notes on the video teaching. The real action will then come as you dig in to each topic during a guided small group experience. During this time your group will be invited to participate in a practical activity designed to move the session's lesson from your head to your heart. This section is called "Living from Victory," and it will serve as a place where the big ideas of this study take on some flesh-and-blood reality.

If you want to get the most out of your experience in this study, you need to keep a couple of things in mind. First, the real growth will happen during your small group time. This is where you will process the content of the message, ask questions, and learn from others as you listen to what God is doing in their lives. This leads to point two: As much as small groups can be a deeply rewarding time of intimacy and friendship, they can also be a disaster. Work to make your group a "safe place." That means both being honest about your thoughts and feelings as well as listening carefully to everyone else's opinion. Third, resist the temptation to "fix" a problem people might be experiencing or to correct their theology. That's not what this time is for. Finally, keep everything your group shares confidential. All this will foster a rewarding sense of community in your group and give God space to do something new in your life.

The great news is it's not God's plan for you to live with some big giant standing in the middle of your life, demoralizing you day by day by day. These giants harm you and rob God of his glory in your life. And it's critical to understand that your freedom and God's glory are forever interwoven into one beautiful story. God wants you to live free. God wants your giants to fall. He wants you to live in liberty and abundance and hope and trust. This is the great outcome that God offers to you.

Goliath MUST fall.

How to Use This Guide

Goliath Must Fall is designed to be as personal as is it practical. Each session begins with an "icebreaker" question followed by a reflection from the Bible. Then you'll watch the video with Louie Giglio and jump into some directed small-group discussion. Even though there are a number of questions available, don't feel like you have to use them all. Your leader will focus on the ones that resonate most with your group and guide you from there.

The final component of each session is called "Living from Victory." In this part of the study, your group will engage in a practical exercise to help you move the content of the session from your head to your heart. Think of this time as an answer to the question, "What am I supposed to *do* with this message?" The goal is to complete these exercises during your meeting time, and they will be what you make of them. If you choose to only go through the motions, or if you refrain from participating, there is less chance you'll find what you're looking for in this study. But if you stay open and give it a chance, you may discover what many others have found to be true: faith comes alive when we take holy risks for God.

Now, it is understandable if the thought of "risky" activities makes you feel anxious. That's okay. If you fall into this category, just read ahead to each "Living from Victory" section, and you will know not only what's coming up but also how to prepare yourself accordingly. Finally, remember that none of these activities involves anything inappropriate or embarrassing. They are just hands-on opportunities to keep you open to God's love and help you see the gospel as true good news.

Following your group time, there will be three more opportunities for you to engage the content during the week. The first activity focuses on something you can *do* to put into practice what you are learning. It is called "Act." The second is called "Worship" and offers a creative way for you to draw closer to God so that he can take charge in overcoming your giant. The third, called "Proclaim," sends you out to share with a friend something you have learned. The challenge will be to do at least one of these activities between sessions and to use this study guide to record what you learn.

Starting in session 2, there will be time before the video to check in about the previous week's activity and process your experiences as a group. Don't worry if you are unable to do an activity one week or are just joining the study. It will still be beneficial for you to hear from the other participants in the group and learn about what they discovered during the week.

Remember the real growth in this study will happen during your small-group time. This is where you will process the content of the message, ask questions, and learn from others as you listen to what God is doing in their lives. The videos, discussions, and activities in this study are simply meant to kick-start your imagination so you are open not only to what God wants you to hear but also how to apply that truth to your life. Just consider what God could do with a whole group of people who were surrendered to him, deep into worship, and experiencing victory over the oppressive giants in their lives. Let's jump into *Goliath Must Fall* and find out.

Note: If you are a group leader, there are additional instructions and resources in the back of this guide to help you lead your members through the study. Because some of the activities require materials and setup, make sure you read this section so you will be prepared.

Dead but Still Deadly

Be alert and of sober mind. Your enemy the devil prowls around like a roaring lion looking for someone to devour. Resist him, standing firm in the faith, because you know that the family of believers throughout the world is undergoing the same kind of sufferings.

1 PETER 5:8-9

Orientation

When Louie was a college student, he worked summers at a church camp on a rustic, jungle-esque island off the coast of South Carolina. One of his jobs was to deal with the poisonous snakes and ensure they didn't become too much of a problem on the path to the bathhouse. Louie and some of the camp counselors would wallop a snake on the head with a baseball bat until it was dead. Then they'd hold the head down with the bat and pull on the snake's body until the head popped off. Finally, they'd grind the head down into the sand and bury it with more sand.

Why bury the head? Because even though the snake was dead, there was still enough venom in its fangs to poison anyone who happened to walk by and step on them. The snake's head was *dead but still deadly*.

That's a good picture of our enemy, Satan. Jesus defeated him on the cross. The battle is over, the victory won. Because of Jesus' death, burial, and resurrection Satan is nothing but a beaten snake with his head torn off. And yet, if we step unwarily on his dead head, those spring-loaded fangs can cause grave harm. If we listen to him or give in to his schemes, we'll get a jab of his crippling venom. It will poison the robust life we are meant to have in Christ.

This week in *Goliath Must Fall*, we'll see this double truth in action. We will explore how on the one hand, Jesus defeated Satan dead on the cross; but on the other hand, that dead serpent's head still has venom. It can still cause serious damage and destruction in our lives.

Pretty much all of us have an area in our lives where Satan threatens to rob our joy and steamroll our capacity to love others. It might be fear, rejection, anger, addiction, or even comfort. We need to know that in Christ, the enemy is dead. We also need Jesus' help to stop stepping on those poison-filled fangs. We need both. In the course of this series, you will discover how to walk in the victory that Jesus has won and keep from falling prey to the giants that rise up to oppose us. We'll discover that we're called to live from that victory, not for it.

When we look at the account of David and Goliath, we often assume that we are David in the story. We think that if we can just muster enough courage and willpower, we can overcome the enemy through our own efforts. But the truth is that Jesus represents David in this story, and we can only truly overcome the enemy when we rely on his strength, not our own.

Isn't that a huge relief?

Welcome and Checking In

Welcome to the first session of *Goliath Must Fall*. If you or any of your fellow group members do not know one another, take a few minutes to introduce yourselves. Then, to get things started, discuss one of the following questions:

- *How have you changed in the past five years?*

or

- *How would you like to change in the next five years?*

Hearing the Word

Read aloud in the group the following passage from 1 Samuel 17:1–9. This is a familiar story, so as you read listen for any fresh insights and write them down to share with the group.

> ¹ Now the Philistines gathered their forces for war and assembled at Sokoh in Judah. They pitched camp at Ephes Dammim, between Sokoh and Azekah. ² Saul and the

Israelites assembled and camped in the Valley of Elah and drew up their battle line to meet the Philistines. [3] The Philistines occupied one hill and the Israelites another, with the valley between them.

[4] A champion named Goliath, who was from Gath, came out of the Philistine camp. His height was six cubits and a span. [5] He had a bronze helmet on his head and wore a coat of scale armor of bronze weighing five thousand shekels; [6] on his legs he wore bronze greaves, and a bronze javelin was slung on his back. [7] His spear shaft was like a weaver's rod, and its iron point weighed six hundred shekels. His shield bearer went ahead of him.

[8] Goliath stood and shouted to the ranks of Israel, "Why do you come out and line up for battle? Am I not a Philistine, and are you not the servants of Saul? Choose a man and have him come down to me. [9] If he is able to fight and kill me, we will become your subjects; but if I overcome him and kill him, you will become our subjects and serve us."

In groups of two or three, share your answers to the following questions:

What was one thing that stood out to you from the Scripture, and why?

How easy is it for you to think of yourself as David in this story, going up against the Goliath in your life? Why did you answer the way you did?

What do you think we are meant to learn from this story?

Watch the Video

Play the video segment for session one. Use the following outline to record any thoughts or concepts that stand out to you.

Notes

It's not God's will for us to have "giants" in our lives that are demoralizing us and stealing God's glory from us.

Our enemy is like a snake without a head—dead but still deadly. He has been defeated at the cross, but there is still poison in his fangs.

Just as in David's day, the enemy will send giants against us to torment us and make us miserable. We can't allow those giants to have power in our lives.

We often view David and Goliath as the classic underdog story. The message we often take away from the story is that if we try hard enough, we can overcome any giant.

But we are not "David" in the story. We can't bring our giants down by trying harder. *Jesus* represents David, and he is the one who does the work in bringing Goliath down.

When Jesus sets us free, we are free indeed (see John 8:36).

David wasn't motivated simply by his own personal freedom. He was motivated to defeat Goliath so he could bring glory and fame to God.

If there is a giant with its foot on our neck, God is not getting the glory in our lives. This is why any Goliath that comes against us *must fall.*

Group Discussion

Take a few minutes with your group members to discuss what you just watched and explore these concepts in Scripture.

1. What do you think is meant by living *from* victory as opposed to living *for* it? How might that play out in your life?

2. How do you respond to the notion that Jesus, not you, is the David who has defeated the giant in your life? What are the implications of this for the way you live your life?

3. Jesus has been given "all authority in heaven and on earth" (Matthew 28:18). The reason Jesus came to earth was to crush the power of sin and death. What difference does this make as to how you view the giant in your life?

4. If Jesus has all authority and has defeated the enemy, and if he wants us to have life to the full, why do you suppose he lets the problems in our lives still have the venom to harm us? How does God's glory figure into the situation?

5. How do you go about drawing close to Jesus so that you won't step on the venomous head of a dead snake?

6. Our ultimate defense against the enemy is leaning into the all-sufficiency of Christ. What does his all-sufficiency mean? How can we lean into it?

Living from Victory

For this activity, each participant will need a blank sheet of paper and a pen.

In this session, you have explored the idea that Jesus, not you, is the David who has brought down your Goliath. Your enemy is dead but still deadly, and your hope is in the all-sufficiency of Jesus. Your power to change isn't in Christ-plus-something. It's in Christ-plus-nothing.

On your blank sheet of paper, make a list of things you tend to rely on to make your life work the way you want it to work. Include things about you (your intelligence, your willpower, your determination) and people or things outside you (your phone, your spouse, your money). You may wish to put Jesus on this list—but for now, list only the *things* and *people* you rely on to have as abundant a life as possible.

When everyone is finished writing, the leader will instruct you to tear up the piece of paper. As you do, offer these items up to God and choose to rely on him alone as your source of strength in life. Say a silent prayer that you desire to start living as though you have Christ-plus-nothing—leaning on him instead of yourself.

Closing Prayer

Close the session by praying the words of Psalm 18:1-6, 13-19, and 46-48 together. You can pray it in unison, or you can let your leader say the odd-numbered verses and the group members say the even-numbered verses.

> [1] I love you, LORD, my strength.
> [2] The LORD is my rock, my fortress and my deliverer;
>   my God is my rock, in whom I take refuge,
>   my shield and the horn of my salvation, my stronghold.

[3] I called to the LORD, who is worthy of praise,
  and I have been saved from my enemies.
[4] The cords of death entangled me;
  the torrents of destruction overwhelmed me.
[5] The cords of the grave coiled around me;
  the snares of death confronted me.
[6] In my distress I called to the LORD;
  I cried to my God for help.
From his temple he heard my voice;
  my cry came before him, into his ears. . . .

[13] The LORD thundered from heaven;
  the voice of the Most High resounded.
[14] He shot his arrows and scattered the enemy,
  with great bolts of lightning he routed them.
[15] The valleys of the sea were exposed
  and the foundations of the earth laid bare
at your rebuke, LORD,
  at the blast of breath from your nostrils.
[16] He reached down from on high and took hold of me;
  he drew me out of deep waters.
[17] He rescued me from my powerful enemy,
  from my foes, who were too strong for me.
[18] They confronted me in the day of my disaster,
  but the LORD was my support.
[19] He brought me out into a spacious place;
  he rescued me because he delighted in me. . . .

[46] The LORD lives! Praise be to my Rock!
  Exalted be God my Savior!
[47] He is the God who avenges me,
  who subdues nations under me,
[48] who saves me from my enemies.

Session One

You are invited to further explore the material you've covered this week by engaging in any or all of the following between-sessions activities. Remember, this part of the *Goliath Must Fall* experience is not about following rules or doing your homework. Rather these activities—called *Act*, *Worship*, and *Proclaim*—will help you take concrete steps toward deeper connection with Jesus so that he can take down the giant in your life. *Be sure to read the reflection questions after each activity and make a few notes in your guide about the experience.* There will be a time for you to share these reflections at the beginning of the next session.

Act: Write a Letter

Write a letter to Jesus about his all-sufficiency, using either a separate sheet of paper or your journal. You can express questions you still have about what it means. You can thank him for being enough to defeat Satan and everything that comes against you. You can confess to him the other things you often turn to for dealing with the challenges in your life. Tell him any areas of your life where you're struggling, and ask him to help you know that he is all-sufficient for these concerns. You can talk with him about any of the ways you are experiencing the deadliness of your enemy, and ask him to help you know that your enemy is really dead for good.

Feel free to be entirely candid and blunt with what you write. If you aren't yet able to understand that he is all-sufficient for everything life throws at you, say so. The psalmists were very blunt in the way they poured out their hearts to the Lord.

Make a few notes about what it was like to write this letter to share with your group next week.

Giants come in all shapes and sizes, some subtle and others stark. The good news is it's not God's plan for you to live with *anything* standing in the middle of your life, demoralizing you day by day by day. These giants harm you and rob God of his glory in your life. God wants you to live free. God wants your giants to fall. He wants you to live without the chains that bind you, unfettered from beliefs that limit you. And you can!
—*Goliath Must Fall*, page xiv

Worship: Offer Your Body

One of the best things you can do to give God full access to your life and your heart is to worship him. Worship puts you in an open posture so that the Holy Spirit can go to work in the deep places of your soul. In Romans 12:1, the apostle Paul writes, "Therefore, I urge you, brothers and sisters, in view of God's mercy, to offer your bodies as a living sacrifice, holy and pleasing to God—this is your true and proper worship." So, for today's worship experience, you're going to offer your body to God.

Stand with your arms outstretched. Beginning with your feet, offer the parts of your body to God as instruments of righteousness (see Romans 6:13). Pray aloud if possible. Say something like, "Jesus, I offer my feet to you. Let them take me only into places that are pleasing to you. Help me to walk as you walk. The gospel of peace is like my stabilizing and protective boot (see Ephesians 6:15). I offer my legs to you. Let them support me as I stand firm in faith and as I run in the pathway of your commands."

Pay particular attention to parts of your body that are related to ways you've experienced the continued deadliness of your enemy. For example, if you've struggled with negative thoughts, address that when you offer your mind to God so that you can focus on "whatever is true, whatever is noble, whatever is right, whatever is pure, whatever is lovely, whatever is admirable" (Philippians 4:8).

Take your time. When you're finished, allow a couple of minutes to rest in God's presence.

Take note of how God uses this activity to speak to you. Write a few sentences about it below to share with the group next week.

God doesn't want us to be demoralized if we face more than one giant that needs to be taken down. He's able to take them all. . . . Jesus wants to ensure us that he is completely and totally able to take down the giants in our lives. It may look as though the six-fingered, six-toed, furious, foaming, fearless thing coming at us can't be beaten. But through the power of Jesus, whatever needs to be overcome can—and will—come down.

—*Goliath Must Fall*, page 19

Proclaim: Share the News

If you're getting something out of this study, don't keep the news to yourself. One great way to worship God is to proclaim what you know about him to others. "As for me, I will declare this forever; I will sing praise to the God of Jacob" (Psalm 75:9). You might tell a friend what you've learned about David and Goliath or about Jesus' all-sufficiency or about your enemy being dead but still deadly. You might confide in someone about a giant in your life and ask them to pray for you.

Write here a few sentences of what you might share with a friend—believer or nonbeliever.

After you share your insight with someone, make a few notes about how it went so that you can report back to your group next week.

Our ultimate defense against giants—the best defense we have—
is to lean into the all-sufficiency of Jesus. Maybe that's a term you've
heard before—*all-sufficiency*—but you aren't quite sure what it means.
Or maybe the term is brand-new to you. We need to unpack some Scripture
around this great truth: that Jesus is all-sufficient. By *sufficient* we mean
that Jesus is *enough*. He is all we need to fulfill God's greatest purposes for
our lives. Jesus is not deficient in anything. Jesus is not lacking or
inadequate or meager or poor. He's fully competent. He's fully abounding.
Thanks to Jesus, we sit at a banqueting table every day; our cups are
constantly overflowing, and our plates are constantly full.
—*Goliath Must Fall*, page 38

Fear Must Fall

Do not fear, for I have redeemed you; I have summoned you by name; you are mine. When you pass through the waters, I will be with you; and when you pass through the rivers, they will not sweep over you. When you walk through the fire, you will not be burned; the flames will not set you ablaze. For I am the LORD your God, the Holy One of Israel, your Savior.

ISAIAH 43:1-3

Orientation

In May 2016, *The Atlantic* magazine ran a cover story called "The Secret Shame of Middle-Class Americans." The cover photo showed a man with a paper bag over his head. The article said nearly half of all Americans would have trouble coming up with $400 in an emergency. The author admitted that despite his relatively successful writing career, he was one of those people.

The author went on to talk about the anxiety he has lived with for years because of his precarious financial condition. "I know what it is like to dread going to the mailbox, because there will always be new bills to pay but seldom a check with which to pay them."[1] Fear—and the shame of hiding it—have been his constant companions.

Again and again in the Bible we are told *not to fear.* The repetition is necessary because fear and its cousins—worry, stress, and terror—are bigger in our world and our individual realities than any other giant we face. Just as Goliath taunted the Israelites day after day, the giant of fear taunts us each day, telling us that terrible things are going to happen to us and there's nothing we can do about them.

Yet as we learned in session one, the giant of fear is dead, though it can still be deadly. Jesus' resurrection shows us that God has power *even over death itself* and there is nothing that we will ever face that he cannot overcome. We show the world that we serve an all-powerful God when we refuse to give in to fear, when we choose to trust that Jesus has overthrown this giant. In this session, we'll learn concrete steps we can take to develop a deep trust in Jesus.

Welcome and Checking In

Go around the group and invite everyone to answer one of the following questions:

• *How well do you sleep? What are some fears that keep you awake at night?*

or

• *What were you afraid of as a child?*

Last week you were invited to participate in the "Between Sessions" section of the study.

• Did you do one of the activities? If so, which one? If not, why not?

• What are some of the things you wrote down in reflection?

• What did you learn by engaging in these activities?

Hearing the Word

Read aloud in the group the following passage from 1 Samuel 17:10-16. As before, listen for any fresh insights as this portion of the David and Goliath story is read.

¹⁰ Then the Philistine said, "This day I defy the armies of Israel! Give me a man and let us fight each other." ¹¹ On hearing the Philistine's words, Saul and all the Israelites were dismayed and terrified.
¹² Now David was the son of an Ephrathite named Jesse, who was from Bethlehem in Judah. Jesse had eight sons, and in Saul's time he was very old. ¹³ Jesse's three oldest sons had followed Saul to the war: The firstborn was Eliab; the second, Abinadab; and the third, Shammah. ¹⁴ David was the youngest. The three oldest followed Saul,

¹⁵ but David went back and forth from Saul to tend his father's sheep at Bethlehem.

¹⁶ For forty days the Philistine came forward every morning and evening and took his stand.

In groups of two or three, share your answers to the following questions:

What was one thing that stood out to you from the Scripture, and why?

What affect do you think Goliath's words had on the Israelites after hearing his taunts every morning and night for forty days?

Why do you think they refused to act?

Watch the Video

Play the video segment for session two. Use the following outline to record any thoughts or concepts that stand out to you.

Notes

In the Bible, there are 365 verses that say "fear not." That's one verse on fear for every day of the year. There are so many verses on fear because we are a fearful people.

Goliath's taunts worked their way into the Israelites' minds and kept them in fear. We have to ask what message has likewise worked its way into our minds and left us feeling terrorized.

Perhaps we are fearful because of our conditioning. We grew up in a household of fear, and now it is just a way of life for us.

We could be fearful because we are concealing something. We fear that people will discover our secret and learn about "the real me."

We could be fearful because we are controlling. We like things to work a certain way—and when that doesn't happen we give in to fear.

Jesus steps into the valley of our fear and says, "Let me be in charge of your life." In the process, he deals with the things that are causing you to fear.

Fear and faith cannot occupy our minds at the same time. Worship and worry simply cannot occupy the same space.

To deal with the giant of fear, we must name it and then put it into the hands of Jesus—and trust that he will take care of it for us.

Group Discussion

Take a few minutes with your group members to discuss what you just watched and explore these concepts in Scripture.

1. The opposite of fear isn't courage. It's faith. What does faith in Jesus involve when we're up against the giant of fear? What do we need to believe? What do we need to do?

2. What's wrong with concealing our fears from others? And if concealment is a problem, why do we do it?

3. What would make this group a safe place for someone to confess to the specific things that are causing his or her anxiety?

4. What helps us become convinced that God is bigger than our fears and has overcome whatever we fear?

5. What role do praise and worship have in dealing with fear? Why are they so important?

6. What hinders us from focusing on Christ all day long? How can we address those hindrances?

Living from Victory

For this activity, each person will need a blank sheet of paper and a pen or pencil. In addition, the leader will need a cross (any size or type).

Identify your biggest fear. Instead of describing it, draw it on your sheet of paper. Your drawing can be terrible—stick figures are fine. Abstract representations are also fine. Just depict either your biggest fear or yourself when you are fearing that thing.

When everyone has had a chance to draw these fears, share them with the people sitting near you. Tell what you were trying to illustrate.

Put the cross in the middle of the group. One by one, let each person slide his or her portrait of fear under the cross. Take a moment to think about what this represents: Jesus triumphing over your fears through his self-sacrifice.

Closing Prayer

Close the session by praying together these words of David from Psalm 34:4–14:

> ⁴ I sought the LORD, and he answered me;
>   he delivered me from all my fears.
> ⁵ Those who look to him are radiant;
>   their faces are never covered with shame.
> ⁶ This poor man called, and the LORD heard him;
>   he saved him out of all his troubles.
> ⁷ The angel of the LORD encamps around those who fear him,
>   and he delivers them.
> ⁸ Taste and see that the LORD is good;
>   blessed is the one who takes refuge in him.
> ⁹ Fear the LORD, you his holy people,
>   for those who fear him lack nothing.

[10] The lions may grow weak and hungry,
> but those who seek the LORD lack no good thing.

[11] Come, my children, listen to me;
> I will teach you the fear of the LORD.

[12] Whoever of you loves life
> and desires to see many good days,

[13] keep your tongue from evil
> and your lips from telling lies.

[14] Turn from evil and do good;
> seek peace and pursue it.

Note

1. Neal Gabler, "The Secret Shame of Middle-Class Americans," *The Atlantic*, May 2016, pp. 52–63.

Session Two

You are invited to further explore the material you've covered this week in *Goliath Must Fall* by engaging in any or all of the following between-sessions activities. *Be sure to read the reflection questions after each activity and make a few notes in your guide about the experience.* There will be a time for you to share these reflections at the beginning of the next session.

Act: Name that Fear

Name the things you fear. Write them down and name them aloud. List as many or as few as there are. It might be one big thing, or it might be several things. What are you anxious about? What are you worried about?

I'm afraid of _____.

I'm afraid that _____.

I'm worried about _____.

_____ keeps me awake at night.

If you're not sure, if you just have free-floating anxiety, then sit down and write whatever comes into your head for twenty minutes.

After twenty minutes, read what you've written and see if there are any clues to the roots of your anxiety. Another approach is to write these sentences and fill in the blanks:

I need _____.
I want _____.
I hope _____, but _____.
If only _____.

Now that you've identified your fear, get into a posture of prayer. That could be sitting, standing, or getting down on your knees—whatever works for you. Close your eyes and hold your hands out, palms down. Say, "Lord Jesus, I entrust these fears to you." Say your fears aloud and picture them falling from your hands into his. Then turn your palms up and ask to receive whatever Jesus wants to give you in exchange.

Make a few notes about your experience to share with the group next week.

The giant of fear can taunt us, but it doesn't have the ultimate power. Jesus has the ultimate power. Fear may seek to obscure our view of God and crush our confidence. Fear may get a grip on our throats and try to choke the very breath out of us. Fear may yell insults and try to convince us that we're going to live with this giant the rest of our lives. But the giant of fear is already dead. It's done for. It was conquered by Jesus on the cross. In the name of Jesus, the giant of fear must fall.

—*Goliath Must Fall*, page 55

Worship: Memorize These

Memorizing Scripture gives you a powerful weapon to use against a dead giant that is taunting you. When you feel anxiety welling up from your hidden heart, you can counter it with true words in your conscious mind. Write this verse five times, saying it aloud as you write and then saying the whole aloud when you are finished writing:

> I have set the LORD always before me;
>> because He is at my right hand I shall not be moved.
> (Psalm 16:8 NKJV)

Take five minutes alone to sit with this verse and repeat it to yourself. To keep it fresh and see it from new angles, emphasize different words or phrases each time you repeat it. (I have set *the* LORD always before me. I have set the LORD always *before me* . . .)

Post this verse somewhere you will see it multiple times a day. (That's what it means to set the Lord always before you. It means literally going back to him in your mind throughout the day.) You can write it as a note on your phone, and when you get the urge to check social media, you can check your verse instead and read it aloud to yourself in a low voice.

If you master Psalm 16:8 and want to add to your memorized arsenal, try verse 9:

> Therefore my heart is glad and my tongue rejoices;
>   my body also will rest secure. (Psalm 16:9)

Make a few notes about this experience of memorizing Scripture to share with the group next week.

Fortunately, it doesn't need to be that way. We don't need
to accommodate the giant of fear. When we go beneath the surface to
discover the root of fear, that's a good place to start. By the power of God in
us, we examine that root and bring it to Jesus and flow Scripture over it and
through it. We immerse ourselves in the goodness and greatness of God,
and let Jesus shine his light on that root.

—*Goliath Must Fall*, page 60

Proclaim: Tell Someone About Your Fear

If you have identified fears that are taunting you, tell someone. Tell
one trusted person what's bothering you. If they're at all mature in
the faith, they will treat your honesty with respect.

Then after you confess your fear, confess also what you know
about God. Confess that you know he's able to take care of you.
Confess that he is mightier than your fears. You might share
Psalm 16:8 with your friend. You also might share Isaiah 46:9–11
(see below).

If your fear still feels too big to manage, that's fine. Be real
about where you are in this process. But do give airtime to both
truths: the honest truth that you're worried and the highest truth
that God has and will and *must* handle it.

Remember the former things, those of long ago;
    I am God, and there is no other;
    I am God, and there is none like me.
I make known the end from the beginning,
    from ancient times, what is still to come.
I say, "My purpose will stand,
    and I will do all that I please."

From the east I summon a bird of prey;
     from a far-off land, a man to fulfill my purpose.
What I have said, that I will bring about;
     what I have planned, that I will do. (Isaiah 46:9–11)

Make a few notes about this experience to share with the group next week.

Do we want to combat the fear in our lives? The battle is not ours. The battle belongs to the Lord. Jesus has already taken the sling and the stone and slain the giant. The giant of fear has already fallen. The work is already done by Christ on the cross. Our responsibility is to have faith. That's the antidote. God is able. Jesus is enough. When we set our eyes on him, we will not be shaken. We will rest secure.

—*Goliath Must Fall*, page 77

Rejection Must Fall

Those who are led by the Spirit of God are the children of God. The Spirit you received does not make you slaves, so that you live in fear again; rather, the Spirit you received brought about your adoption to sonship. And by him we cry, "Abba, Father." The Spirit himself testifies with our spirit that we are God's children. Now if we are children, then we are heirs—heirs of God and co-heirs with Christ.

ROMANS 8:14-16

Orientation

Rejection letters for writers are legendary. New writers are coached on how to get ready for multifarious rejections from agents and editors. Blogger Nathaniel Tower even goes so far as to categorize rejection letters in his post "Ten Levels of Rejection (and What to Do about Them)."

There even used to be a magazine called *Rejected Quarterly* that accepted only short stories that had been rejected at least five times. Writers submitted the five rejection letters as proof, along with their stories. Sadly, like many magazines in recent years, *Rejected Quarterly* stopped publishing due to lack of interest. It was rejected by its audience.

As painful as writerly rejection is, though, it is dwarfed by the pain of rejection from someone close to us: a parent, a spouse. A few words from a key person in our world, or the lack thereof, can shape our view of ourselves for our entire lives. Rejection looms as a giant and haunts us with its cousins—insecurity, inferiority, perfectionism, or compulsive drivenness. Whenever we believe we're only as good as our latest success (or failure), we're in the clutches of the giant of rejection.

Fortunately, God counters that toxic thinking with the only thing that can defeat it: his acceptance. In this session, we will see how David resisted the pull of rejection and how God invites us to embrace the acceptance he offers us.

Welcome and Checking In

Go around the group and invite everyone to answer one of the following questions:

- *When you were growing up, who accepted you just as you were? (If the answer is nobody, you can say so.)*

or

• *What are some of the ways you typically respond to rejection?*

Last week you were invited to participate in the "Between Sessions" section of the study.

• Did you do one of the activities? If so, which one? If not, why not?

• What are some of the things you wrote down in reflection?

• What did you learn by engaging in these activities?

Hearing the Word

Read aloud in the group the following passage from 1 Samuel 17:32–37. As before, listen for any fresh insights as this portion of the David and Goliath story is read.

³² David said to Saul, "Let no one lose heart on account of this Philistine; your servant will go and fight him."

³³ Saul replied, "You are not able to go out against this Philistine and fight him; you are only a young man, and he has been a warrior from his youth."

³⁴ But David said to Saul, "Your servant has been keeping his father's sheep. When a lion or a bear came and carried off a sheep from the flock, ³⁵ I went after it, struck it and rescued the sheep from its mouth. When it turned on me, I seized it by its hair, struck it and killed it. ³⁶ Your servant has killed both the lion and the bear; this uncircumcised Philistine will be like one of them, because he has defied the armies of the living God. ³⁷ The LORD who

rescued me from the paw of the lion and the paw of the bear will rescue me from the hand of this Philistine."

Saul said to David, "Go, and the LORD be with you."

In groups of two or three, share your answers to the following questions:

What was one thing that stood out to you from the Scripture, and why?

How did Saul react when David offered to fight the giant?

How did David respond to these words of rejection?

Watch the Video

Play the video segment for session three. Use the following outline to record any thoughts or concepts that stand out to you.

Notes

It's often hard to shake off comments said about us—or not said about us. Feeling as if we don't live up to others' expectation can lead to the giant of rejection in our lives.

In life, we have to ask if we are doing things "so that" or "because." Are we doing things *so that* we can get something from God? Or *because* of what God has already done?

The difference in the two phrases is powerful. We do not serve God so that we can somehow gain his approval, but "because he first loved us" (1 John 4:19).

People operating out of a *so that* attitude respond in one of two ways to rejection. They are either crushed and feel unworthy of others' love, or they flip it around and vow to become the best at everything to prove they are somebody worthy of love.

God has already decided that we are "good enough" to have a relationship with us. We were never worthy of this on our own, but we were worth it enough for God to send his Son to die for our sins.

If we live *for* people's approval, we will never feel as if we measure up. But if we live *from* God's approval, we will already know that we are accepted. This mindset changes everything.

The Bible says we are worthy, loved, valued, and chosen sons and daughters of God. The giant of acceptance falls when we choose to live this out.

Rejected people reject people. Loved and accepted people love and accept people. We must believe we are accepted by God to truly accept others—and thus promote God's glory.

Group Discussion

Take a few minutes with your group members to discuss what you just watched and explore these concepts in Scripture.

1. Consider the reasons outlined in the video about why people typically feel rejected. Could you identify with any of them? If so, which ones?

2. What reasons for feeling deeply accepted did you hear in the video? Which of them are already prominent in your thoughts, and which aren't?

3. What does it mean to understand the miracle of our creation? How does that nurture a sense of acceptance?

4. In what sense can you say, "God chose me"? What does this mean to you, and why is it so important?

5. What do you think we need to do to become fully captivated by God's acceptance so that it affects the way we think and act?

6. What's the difference between living *for* acceptance and living *from* it? How can you put this into practice?

Living from Victory

For this exercise, each person will need two blank nametags. They might say in small letters, "I am" or "Hello, my name is _____ " but there needs to be plenty of room for people to write their names. Each person also needs a marker to write with.

On one of your nametags, write a name that you have been called, or that you have called yourself, that is a rejection name. Rejection names include *unworthy; unwanted; broken; irreparable; unloved; outcast; lonely.* Whatever the name is, write it on the tag and place the tag on your arm.

When everyone has done this, the leader will invite the group to call out the acceptance names that God has given to you to overcome these words of rejection. Acceptance names include *worthy; loved; valued; chosen; cherished; son or daughter of God.* List as many of these acceptance names as you can.

Now pair up with a partner other than your spouse. If there's an extra person, make a group of three. On the blank nametag that you still have, write one of the acceptance names. Stick it on your partner over his or her rejection name. Say, "You think your name is [*rejection name*], but your real name is [*acceptance name*]." Then your partner will do the same for you. If you have a group of three, you can go in a circle so that each person has a chance to write an acceptance name and to receive one.

Don't throw away your acceptance name when the group ends. Place it somewhere you will see it daily as a reminder to live from acceptance this week.

Closing Prayer

Close the session by praying together this prayer based on Paul's words in Ephesians 3:16–21:

We pray that out of God's glorious riches he may strengthen us with power through his Spirit in our inner being, so that Christ may dwell in our hearts through faith.

And we pray that we, being rooted and established in love, may have power, together with all the Lord's holy people, to grasp how wide and long and high and deep is the love of Christ, and to know this love that surpasses knowledge—that we may be filled to the measure of all the fullness of God.

Now to him who is able to do immeasurably more than all we ask or imagine, according to his power that is at work within us, to him be glory in the church and in Christ Jesus throughout all generations, for ever and ever! Amen.

Session Three

You are invited to further explore the material you've covered this week in *Goliath Must Fall* by engaging in any or all of the following between-sessions activities. *Be sure to read the reflection questions after each activity and make a few notes in your guide about the experience.* There will be a time for you to share these reflections at the beginning of the next session.

Act: List Your Rejections

It can be helpful to face the times in your life when you felt rejected. What were the big ones? Maybe one or both of your parents rejected you when you were a child. Or maybe rejection by a boyfriend/girlfriend had a lasting impact and affected the way you felt about yourself. Maybe you have endured a divorce. Maybe a close friend turned his or her back on you for reasons you still don't understand. Take time to write down what happened and how it affected you. Nobody will read this except you. Here's a guide:

- I was rejected by _____ when _____.
- What happened was this: _____.
- It left me feeling _____.

Now go a little further and write out some details. Try to dig deeper than "It left me feeling sad," or, "It left me feeling hurt." If you're not a person who normally dwells on feelings, see if you can come up with what it made you do: "It left me not wanting to get up and try again with somebody else."

- It left me not wanting to _____.
- Instead, I wanted to _____.
- What I actually did in response was _____.
- Looking back, I can see that over time my response to this rejection has been _____.

How has rejection affected different areas of your life? For example, are you reluctant to put yourself out there in social environments or work situations because it's safer to be invisible than risk being rejected? Are you highly competitive or easily agitated when you don't win? Or are you excessively driven and determined to win at all cost? What price do others pay for your success?

- Rejection affects the way I _____.
- I make sure I never have to face rejection or failure because _____.
- Some of the things I have done to assure my success are _____.

When you're done writing out your experiences of rejection, make a few notes summarizing your insights to share with the group next week.

We've all felt that we don't measure up. We all experience performance-based environments where we feel we need to work hard or else we won't gain approval. Way back in the Garden of Eden, a seed of rejection was planted in humanity. That seed is a big spiky plant now, and its blooms insist we must compare ourselves with everybody else. See, we all began miraculously—fully loved and fully accepted—in the mind and heart of almighty God. We are all God's creations. Masterpieces. Yet we were born into a fallen world that's bought the lie that people are only worth what they can achieve or what other people say they are worth.

—*Goliath Must Fall*, page 86

Worship: Bask in God's Acceptance

The antidote to being driven by the pain of rejection is to bask in the deep and complete acceptance we have from God. There are a number of Bible passages that might help you do this, such as Romans 8:31–39; Ephesians 1:3–14; 3:16–19. The passage we're going to focus on here is Psalm 8.

An ideal way to reflect on Psalm 8 is to go out for a night walk. If you live in an urban setting where light pollution blots out the night sky, try driving out of the city into an area where you can see the stars the way David saw them. Pick a cloudless night if possible. Look up at the stars—really see them.

If a clear starry night is not available to you, go in the daytime to a place that displays God's majestic handiwork in mountains or great trees or a vast lake or ocean. If none of that is an option, go online and find images of the grandeur of God's handiwork.

Here's the psalm:

> [1] LORD, our Lord,
>   how majestic is your name in all the earth!
> You have set your glory
>   in the heavens.
> [2] Through the praise of children and infants
>   you have established a stronghold against your enemies,
>   to silence the foe and the avenger.
> [3] When I consider your heavens,
>   the work of your fingers,
> the moon and the stars,
>   which you have set in place,
> [4] what is mankind that you are mindful of them,
>   human beings that you care for them?
> [5] You have made them a little lower than the angels
>   and crowned them with glory and honor.
> [6] You made them rulers over the works of your hands;
>   you put everything under their feet:
> [7] all flocks and herds,
>   and the animals of the wild,
> [8] the birds in the sky,
>   and the fish in the sea,
>   all that swim the paths of the seas.
> [9] LORD, our Lord,
>   how majestic is your name in all the earth!

As you read Psalm 8 think about this: God made this incredible creation—all those magnificent stars—and yet he cares for *you*. He has made you a little lower than the angels and crowned you with glory and honor. That's how he sees you: crowned with his own glory. He sees you that way regardless of how much you have succeeded or failed in your life. Compared to the starry heavens you may feel small, but David says no, the night sky makes him amazed that he matters so much to God.

Spend some time rolling these verses around in your head. Let them bump up against your feelings of inferiority or drivenness. Let the sight of God's creation be a permanent reminder to you of how much you matter to him. If your feelings of rejection go back to your childhood, here's a verse to memorize:

> Though my father and mother forsake me, the LORD will receive me. (Psalm 27:10)

Write down a few notes about your time of worship to share with the group next week.

David pressed through the rejection he felt to go on and accomplish the
purposes of God for his life. He arrived at the battle from a place
of *true* acceptance. And this is God's invitation to us as well—to cloak
ourselves in the true acceptance that Christ offers. Whether it's school
or work or with our peers or family, we potentially face rejection
every day. The only thing that will help us move past the giant of rejection
is to immerse ourselves in the acceptance of Christ. We need to arrive
at the battle already feeling accepted.

—*Goliath Must Fall*, page 97

Proclaim: Tell Someone What God Has Done

Tell a friend or coworker you trust about your journey through
Psalm 8 and what it meant to you. Tell them something else you've
learned about God's acceptance. It doesn't have to be long; you can
just say a few sentences and celebrate how God's acceptance has
impacted you.

David ends Psalm 8 with these words: "*LORD*, our Lord, how majestic
is your name in all the earth!" Do you know why he concluded the psalm this
way? It's because the worship of God shuts down the giants. Rejection and
worship cannot exist in the same place. One displaces the other. . . . Our freedom and God's glory are forever wound together in one story. Our giants go
down so that we get free, yes, but they primarily go down so God gets glory.
Let's rediscover the miracle of our creation. Let's revel in the mystery of God
choosing us. Let's wrap our hearts around the huge cost that was paid to
rescue us, and turn our hearts toward the One who's already pursuing us.

—*Goliath Must Fall*, page 106

Comfort Must Fall

—

Then he called the crowd to him along with his disciples and said: "Whoever wants to be my disciple must deny themselves and take up their cross and follow me. For whoever wants to save their life will lose it, but whoever loses their life for me and for the gospel will save it."

MARK 8:34-35

Orientation

In 1785, when Thomas Clarkson was a student at Cambridge University in England, he entered a contest to write the best Latin essay on the topic assigned for that year: "Is It Lawful to Enslave the Unconsenting?" He had rarely thought about the slave trade before then, but his research for the contest essay shattered his complacency on the subject.

After reading the essay aloud to an audience in Cambridge, he couldn't get the subject out of his mind during the trip back to London. He later wrote, "I sat down disconsolate on the turf by the roadside and held my horse. Here a thought came into my mind, that if the contents of the Essay were true, it was time some person should see these calamities to their end."[1]

Clarkson was twenty-four-years-old and without influential connections. Yet he took the first step he could take: he translated his essay into English and self-published it. The essay encouraged people such as William Wilberforce, a member of Parliament, to take up the cause. Clarkson spent the succeeding decades in partnership with Wilberforce and others, digging up firsthand information about the slave trade for their campaign. Along the way, Clarkson became a target for the rich and well-connected slave traders—in Liverpool he was attacked and nearly killed by a group of sailors paid to do the job. Yet he and his comrades persevered, and Britain abolished the slave trade in 1807.

If the twenty-four-year-old Clarkson had given in to his doubts (*I'm a nobody; there's nothing that I can do; the traders are too powerful; opposing them would be too dangerous*), the British slave trade might have gone on decades longer than it did. In this session we'll consider how a sneaky, yet prevalent, giant called Comfort can keep us from stepping out in faith in the ways God is calling us to, and we'll see how that giant has been defeated in our lives.

Our job isn't whipping up our courage; it's remembering some key facts: *Life is short. God is big.*

Welcome and Checking In

Go around the group and invite everyone to answer one of the following questions:

* *When was a time that you had to put aside personal comfort in order to do something that God had for you to do?*

or

* *If money, time, and influence were no barriers, what would you like to see God do through you?*

Last week you were invited to participate in the "Between Sessions" section of the study.

* Did you do one of the activities? If so, which one? If not, why not?

* What are some of the things you wrote down in reflection?

* What did you learn by engaging in these activities?

Hearing the Word

Read aloud in the group the following passage from 1 Samuel 17:17–25. As before, listen for any fresh insights as this portion of the David and Goliath story is read.

[17] Now Jesse said to his son David, "Take this ephah of roasted grain and these ten loaves of bread for your brothers and hurry to their camp. [18] Take along these ten cheeses to the commander of their unit. See how your brothers are and bring back some assurance from them. [19] They are with

Saul and all the men of Israel in the Valley of Elah, fighting against the Philistines."

[20] Early in the morning David left the flock in the care of a shepherd, loaded up and set out, as Jesse had directed. He reached the camp as the army was going out to its battle positions, shouting the war cry. [21] Israel and the Philistines were drawing up their lines facing each other. [22] David left his things with the keeper of supplies, ran to the battle lines and asked his brothers how they were. [23] As he was talking with them, Goliath, the Philistine champion from Gath, stepped out from his lines and shouted his usual defiance, and David heard it. [24] Whenever the Israelites saw the man, they all fled from him in great fear.

[25] Now the Israelites had been saying, "Do you see how this man keeps coming out? He comes out to defy Israel. The king will give great wealth to the man who kills him. He will also give him his daughter in marriage and will exempt his family from taxes in Israel."

In groups of two or three, share your answers to the following questions:

What was one thing that stood out to you from the Scripture, and why?

What was the Israelites' situation in the Valley of Elah?

How do you think this might have led to their complacency in facing Goliath?

Watch the Video

Play the video segment for session four. Use the following outline to record any thoughts or concepts that stand out to you.

Notes

The Christian life is not a spectator sport. It's not about sitting in a comfortable church celebrating a Savior who led an uncomfortable life.

Jesus did not come to live an easy life and retire in luxury. He came to fulfill a purpose, and he calls us to fulfill the mission that he gave to us.

David accomplished in forty minutes what the entire Israelite army couldn't accomplish in forty days. The men were not motivated to go into battle because they had tents, food, and supplies—in a word, they were *comfortable*.

Our faith thrives in discomfort. No one in Scripture who played a significant role in God's plan ever did so by choosing the easy route, living in ease, or refusing to take a risk.

The cross—the supreme example of difficulty and suffering—is where the gospel is unpacked in all its power. God chose the difficult path of sending his Son to die on our behalf.

Faith flourishes in hostile territory because it is countercultural. God moves among his people when they are willing to step out of their comfort zone and pursue his plans.

It is in the soil of discomfort that the seeds of the gospel most often flourish.

We sign up to be partners with God when we choose to be where Jesus is—and go wherever that leads us. As we do, the layers of comfort fade away, and the giant of comfort falls.

Group Discussion

Take a few minutes with your group members to discuss what you just watched and explore these concepts in Scripture.

1. Why is comfort a dangerous giant? How can it affect us for the worse?

2. On a scale of 0 to 5, how important is comfort to you? Why did you answer the way you did? How does your desire for comfort play itself out in your daily life?

3. Can you see any areas in which your desire for comfort is limiting what you might do for God? If so, what are those areas?

4. The point of our lives is the fame of Jesus. How can our lives proclaim the fame of Jesus?

5. "Life is short. God is big." How would you explain each of those statements in your own words? Why are they important to remember together?

6. What might it look like for you to get out of your comfort zone in order to serve God in some way? How do you feel about that?

Living from Victory

For this activity, the leader will need something to write on that the whole group can see: a flip chart, a sheet of butcher paper taped to the wall, or a whiteboard. The leader will also need a marker to write with.

As a group, take some time to brainstorm a list of attributes that Jesus and David had that are the opposite of comfort seeking. For example: *passionate, bold, generous, selfless, initiative, purpose-driven,* and *missional.* The leader will write these attributes on the whiteboard, butcher paper, or flip chart.

Next, the leader will ask everyone in the group to complete one of these sentences:

If I were _____ like Jesus,
then I would _____.

If I were _____ like Jesus,
then I wouldn't have to _____.

For example, "If I were generous like Jesus, then I would give sacrificially of my time for the work of God's kingdom." "If I were missional like Jesus, then I wouldn't avoid initiating significant conversations with the people at work."

When everyone has had a chance to complete the sentence, the leader will ask participants to share one risk they are going to take based on these truths about who they are in Christ. "This week I'm going to step out of my comfort zone and follow Jesus into this risk: _____." Encourage everyone to speak aloud one risk in front of the group.

Closing Prayer

Close the session by reading this prayer based on Paul's words in Philippians 1:20–21, 27–29:

Lord, today we pray that you will give us the courage to step out of our comfort zones and step away from our comfortable lives to bring glory to Christ. Regardless of what we face, we pray that you will be continually exalted in our midst. Help us to always conduct ourselves in a manner worthy of the gospel. And let us stand firm together, so that we may overcome those who come against us. Thank you, Lord, that you have saved us and rescued us from our sins. Help us to remember your example and follow you wherever you lead us. Amen.

Note

1. Thomas Clarkson, *The History of the Rise, Progress, and Accomplishment of the Abolition of the African Slave-Trade by the British Parliament*, vol. 1 (London: 1808). Project Gutenberg, http://www.gutenberg.org/cache/epub/12428/pg12428.html.

Session Four

You are invited to further explore the material you've covered this week in *Goliath Must Fall* by engaging in any or all of the following between-sessions activities. *Be sure to read the reflection questions after each activity and make a few notes in your guide about the experience.* There will be a time for you to share these reflections at the beginning of the next session.

Act: Living Beyond Comfort

Do at least one thing this week that stretches you as you seek to boldly follow Jesus. Here are a few possibilities:

- Do a random act of kindness (see the ideas at https://www.randomactsofkindness.org/kindness-ideas).
- Do a non-random act of kindness, helping out someone (an elderly neighbor, for example) who could use the help. Rake their leaves, shovel their snow, return their trashcans from the curb to the garage. (Before you act, ask them what would be most helpful.)
- Invite someone to church.

- Make a donation to a ministry that advocates for the "least of these."
- Tell someone in your life, other than your spouse or significant other, that you love them.
- Tell a nonbeliever something that you have learned from *Goliath Must Fall.*
- Ask someone how you can pray for them. If you're already comfortable doing that with believers, ask a nonbeliever.
- Write a handwritten thank-you note to someone who has been kind to you or supported you in some way. Or make a phone call or face-to-face visit with a family member to say thank you. (No texting or emailing.)
- Serve at a homeless shelter.

Write a few sentences about your experience outside your comfort zone to share with your group at your next meeting.

Comfort is perhaps the scariest giant of them all. It's so subtle in its deception. It's the giant that causes us to miss the very best because we have settled for something good. . . . Sometimes it's not the overtly horrible things that kill us. We aren't heroin addicts. We aren't going to prison for tax evasion. On the contrary, we are honest and honorable. Yet have just settled for comfort, and the comfort ends up doing us in. Our abundant life on earth and our eternal reward in heaven aren't robbed by the "bad" stuff. Our chance for a meaningful life and a happy forever is robbed by comfort.
—*Goliath Must Fall*, pages 111–113

Worship: Chew on This

The apostle Paul had a lifestyle of living an all-in existence for Jesus. Again and again he was arrested and beaten for spreading the word about Jesus. He hiked across the mountainous and desolate terrain of what is modern-day Turkey; he was shipwrecked several times; he went hungry and cold. Here is something he wrote to some friends in the town of Philippi:

> I want to know Christ—yes, to know the power of his resurrection and participation in his sufferings, becoming like him in his death, and so, somehow, attaining to the resurrection from the dead. Not that I have already obtained all this, or have already arrived at my goal, but I press on to take hold of that for which Christ Jesus took hold of me. (Philippians 3:10–12)

If comfort has a strong pull in your life, spend some time reflecting on this passage. You might commit to memory verses 10–11, or you might zero in on the phrase "participation in his sufferings." In what ways might Jesus want you to share in his sufferings, taking a risk for the sake of the gospel? Or you might focus on the phrase "I press on." How can you press on to take hold of what Jesus offers, as opposed to passively waiting for life to fall into your lap? Choose a phrase or a sentence that you can use as a weapon against that dead giant of comfort.

If you're uncomfortable with the phrase you've chosen, that's great! Spend ten minutes with it anyway, chewing on its meaning for your life. Thank God for what he's teaching you. Offer him some worship about it. Maybe you've got more questions than answers about it at this point. Maybe you don't feel ready to take the step you think Jesus is calling you to take. That's fine. For now, just sit with your uncomfortable phrase and let it soak into your mind and raise your heart toward Christ.

Finally, write your phrase as a note on your phone. For the next week, every time you check your phone for messages, check in with your phrase as a message from God to you. Think about how it applies to you at that moment.

Make a few notes about this experience of reflecting on Scripture to share with the group next week.

A nest is a good thing for a while. It's safe and comfortable and sheltered, and all our spiritual baby-needs are taken care of. But if we're not careful, then the giant of comfort tempts us to stay in the nest forever. Maybe we're worried about leaving the nest. We see a big dog below on the ground. We're not sure if we can fly or not. But staying in the nest is never our end goal. Comfort and familiarity are not what God points us toward. Jesus isn't in the business of flying to and fro for the rest of our lives, hand-delivering spiritual baby food to us. The calling of faith pushes us out of the nest. Jesus says, "Hey, you weren't made to live in the nest forever. You were made to live out in a broken world where there's conflict and risk." The gospel of Jesus pushes us out of the nest and says, "You're ready to fly. Off you go."

—*Goliath Must Fall*, pages 114–116

Proclaim: Talk to Someone

Tell someone what you've learned about yourself and comfort this week. Instead of telling a close friend, challenge yourself to talk to someone at work, or a parent of your child's friend, or someone else you know less well.

You could simply say, "I'm taking a class, and we've been learning about the natural tendency to play it safe and not take risks. I have learned about myself that _____." You could even ask, "Have you ever thought about what living a bold life looks like?" Listen to their response and take it as an opportunity to deepen a relationship.

The point of this exercise is to develop your experience of talking about your faith naturally with the people in your life. You're not dumping the whole truck of the gospel on someone, but you're providing openings where a spiritual conversation could occur if the other person signals willingness.

Make a few notes about this experience to share with the group next week.

God will accomplish his plans one way or another, yet God is inviting you to be part of his plans. It won't always be comfortable. It won't always be easy. You will probably need to step forward, not knowing anything other than you're far out with God on the end of the limb, believing that he wants to make his fame known to this generation of people. Yet if you move in faith, God will always breathe life on your journey.

—*Goliath Must Fall*, pages 131–132

Anger Must Fall

My dear brothers and sisters, take note of this: Everyone should be quick to listen, slow to speak and slow to become angry, because human anger does not produce the righteousness that God desires. Therefore, get rid of all moral filth and the evil that is so prevalent and humbly accept the word planted in you, which can save you.

JAMES 1:19-21

Orientation

Do you ever wonder why the world seems to be so full of angry people? It may be because anger, whether overt or buried, has a payoff for the angry person.

Psychologist Leon Seltzer says that when we feel angry, our brains secrete the hormone norepinephrine, which is a painkiller.[1] The anger thus helps us to numb whatever other feeling triggered it. That numbed feeling may be fear or hurt or the pain of rejection or many other possibilities. Anger makes us feel like we're in control—even when we're losing control of the anger.

But many of us, especially Christians, have been taught that it's not okay to get angry. So instead of exploding in rage, we bury our anger. We smile and say that we've forgiven those who hurt us when really we've only minimized the degree of pain the hurt has caused us. We say that we're "over it" when deep down we're not over it at all. The very thought of letting the other person off the hook for what he or she did fills us with a tough, stubborn "no." We want that person to pay a price for the wrongdoing.

Wanting the other person to pay the just consequences of his or her actions is at the very heart of anger. And in itself, there's nothing wrong with that longing for justice. God is a God of justice, so going to him with our anger is the best thing we could possibly do with it.

In this session we will come to grips with our anger and look at what's involved in dealing with it positively. We will talk to ourselves about our anger the way God talks to us, acknowledging that we aren't perfect and yet God has reconciled us to himself. God wants to be our avenger while we let go of the demand to make the other person pay.

Even though anger can feel good in the moment, unexpressed or wrongly expressed anger harms us and others. We don't have to be stuck with that harm.

Freedom is at hand.

Welcome and Checking In

Go around the group and invite everyone to answer one of these questions:

- *How was anger dealt with in your family when you were growing up?*

or

- *If one of your friends said something that really angered you, would you more likely speak up at the time, say nothing, or secretly plan to retaliate?*

Last week you were invited to participate in the "Between Sessions" section of the study.

- Did you do one of the activities? If so, which one? If not, why not?

- What are some of the things you wrote down in reflection?

- What did you learn by engaging in these activities?

Hearing the Word

Read aloud in the group the following passage from 1 Samuel 17:26–31. As before, listen for any fresh insights as this portion of the David and Goliath story is read.

26 David asked the men standing near him, "What will be done for the man who kills this Philistine and removes this disgrace from Israel? Who is this uncircumcised Philistine that he should defy the armies of the living God?"

[27] They repeated to him what they had been saying and told him, "This is what will be done for the man who kills him."

[28] When Eliab, David's oldest brother, heard him speaking with the men, he burned with anger at him and asked, "Why have you come down here? And with whom did you leave those few sheep in the wilderness? I know how conceited you are and how wicked your heart is; you came down only to watch the battle."

[29] "Now what have I done?" said David. "Can't I even speak?" [30] He then turned away to someone else and brought up the same matter, and the men answered him as before. [31] What David said was overheard and reported to Saul, and Saul sent for him.

In groups of two or three, share your answers to the following questions:

What was one thing that stood out to you from the Scripture, and why?

How did Eliab try to provoke David? What anger does he seem to have against David? How did David respond to his brother?

Watch the Video

Play the video segment for session five. Use the following outline to record any thoughts or concepts that stand out to you.

Notes

Anger has a tendency to simmer beneath the surface of our lives and then suddenly burst into flames when something provokes us.

Adolescents in society today are crippled by anxiety. They live in a cauldron of stimuli that they can't get away from, don't want to get away from, or don't know how to get away from.

When David came to the battlefield and started asking questions about Goliath, it caused his brother Eliab to fire angry darts at him. He first questioned David's motives about coming there.

Our anger is provoked when people question our motives. David's brother Eliab did this when he asked David his reasons for coming to the battlefield.

Our anger is provoked when others belittle us. Eliab did this when he asked David with whom he left "those few sheep in the desert."

Our anger is provoked when people attack our character. Eliab did this when he told David he was conceited and wicked and had only come to watch the battle.

There are several different forms of anger:

Wrongly placed anger:

Rightly placed anger:

Suppressed anger:

When we go to the cross, we focus on our own imperfections (we have wronged God as well) and allow the Lord to be the avenger of our wrongs.

Group Discussion

Take a few minutes with your group members to discuss what you just watched and explore these concepts in Scripture.

1. What was wrong with Eliab's anger? Can you identify with him in any ways? If so, how?

2. Sometimes we're angry for a genuine wrong done to us. Based on the teaching you just heard, what would you say is a healthy way of dealing with that anger?

3. What's your usual way of dealing with anger? (If you're never angry, that's a way of dealing with it.) How do you respond when a goal of yours is blocked?

4. Is it helpful for you to think of God as your avenger? Why did you answer as you did?

5. Forgiveness means acknowledging the wrong done but not holding it against the other person. How readily do you forgive? Are there people you find it hard to forgive? If so, why?

6. What helps you know that you are a loved son or daughter of God? How does knowing that help you forgive?

Living from Victory

For this activity, the group will need at least one backpack fully loaded with heavy items such as books, rocks, or bottles of water. If you have a large group, you may want more than one backpack. Consider having a heavier backpack for the men and a lighter-but-still-challenging backpack for the women.

Anger is a physical emotion, and this exercise is designed to put you in touch with the physicality of anger.

Ask for a volunteer to put on the backpack. Next, ask that person to adopt the physical signs of anger: Tense your jaw, furrow your brows, squint your eyes, ball up your fists, and tense your biceps. Your facial expression should be just short of a lion-like growl. With your body and face in this state, practice walking across the room and back again. This is what it's like to carry anger around with you all day.

When that person has had a minute or so to feel the weight of anger, have him or her give the backpack to the next volunteer. This person should put on the backpack and adopt the angry expression. Repeat until all group members have had a chance to wear the backpack and the angry body language. Those with back problems can skip the backpack and just do the angry body language.

When everyone has had a chance to experience the weight and the angry grimace, take a few minutes to debrief:

- What would it be like to walk around like that all day?

- What did it feel like to take off the backpack and let go of the angry body language?

- If it feels so good to let our bodies relax, why do you suppose we so often hold on to anger and refuse to forgive?

Closing Prayer

To close, read aloud Psalm 32.

[1] Blessed is the one
    whose transgressions are forgiven,
    whose sins are covered.
[2] Blessed is the one
    whose sin the LORD does not count against them
    and in whose spirit is no deceit.
[3] When I kept silent,
    my bones wasted away
    through my groaning all day long.
[4] For day and night
    your hand was heavy on me;
my strength was sapped
    as in the heat of summer.
[5] Then I acknowledged my sin to you
    and did not cover up my iniquity.
I said, "I will confess
    my transgressions to the LORD."
And you forgave
    the guilt of my sin.
[6] Therefore let all the faithful pray to you
    while you may be found;

surely the rising of the mighty waters
>   will not reach them.
[7] You are my hiding place;
>   you will protect me from trouble
>   and surround me with songs of deliverance.
[8] I will instruct you and teach you in the way you should go;
>   I will counsel you with my loving eye on you.
[9] Do not be like the horse or the mule,
>   which have no understanding
but must be controlled by bit and bridle
>   or they will not come to you.
[10] Many are the woes of the wicked,
>   but the LORD's unfailing love
>   surrounds the one who trusts in him.
[11] Rejoice in the LORD and be glad, you righteous;
>   sing, all you who are upright in heart!

Note

1. Leon F. Seltzer, "What Your Anger May Be Hiding," *Psychology Today*, July 11, 2008, https://www.psychologytoday.com/blog/evolution-the-self/200807/what-your-anger-may-be-hiding.

Session Five

You are invited to further explore the material you've covered this week in *Goliath Must Fall* by engaging in any or all of the following between-sessions activities. *Be sure to read the reflection questions after each activity and make a few notes in your guide about the experience.* There will be a time for you to share these reflections at the beginning of the next session.

Act: Take an Inventory

Take a self-inventory. As you work through the list below, does anything stick out at you as something you're angry about? Circle the statements that bear the most weight in your life.

The list uses "parent" a lot, but you can put someone else in the story. A friend. A coworker. A boss. A grandparent. An ex-boyfriend or girlfriend. A brother or sister. A coach. A teacher. A pastor. An industry. An institution. A country. A government. A terrorist. The circumstances of life. God. You feel betrayed or belittled or cheated. You wanted something but didn't get it.

If you have trouble identifying with the word *angry*, think about other words for it, such as *annoyed, irritated, bitter*, or *frustrated*.

Circle as many as apply, and write in names or other information in the blanks if you feel comfortable doing so. No one need see this but you.

- _____ hurt me.
- _____ abandoned me.
- _____ wasn't interested in me.
- _____ picked somebody or something else over me.
- _____, who I cared about, was emotionally unavailable to me.
- _____ left my family.
- My dad/mom cheated on us. He/she didn't just cheat on my other parent, he/she cheated on all of us.
- My parent lives with another family.
- I'm angry because other kids get my parent's attention every day.
- I'm angry because my dad or mom is too busy for me.
- I'm angry with my dad or mom because he/she didn't take care of us.
- I'm angry with my dad or mom because he/she didn't take care of himself/herself.
- I'm angry with _____ because he/she won't face the facts.
- _____ is too aggressive / too passive.
- _____ embarrasses me.
- _____ is gone all the time.
- I'm angry with God because _____ _____.
- I'm angry because I didn't get to say good-bye.
- I'm angry because of all the hurtful things that _____ _____ has called me.

- I'm angry because of all the things that _____
  _____ has said to me.
- I'm angry because of all the things _____
  _____ never said to me.
- I'm angry because _____
  _____.
- I'm angry because _____
  _____.
- I'm angry because _____
  _____.

Now look back at the anger statements you circled. Write a *W* beside the items that are wrongly placed anger. Write an *R* beside the ones that are rightly placed anger. Write an *S* beside the ones that have been suppressed anger in your life—maybe this is the first time you've faced the fact that you feel annoyed or bitter or frustrated about this.

When you're done, take a step back and see what you can learn from the *W*'s, *R*'s, and *S*'s. Is there a pattern to your anger?

Make a few notes about what it was like to try to identify who you're angry at and why.

Anger is not wrong. But if anger is uncontrolled, stuffed, misplaced, or given full vent, then anger can do us a lot of harm. Scripture is clear that anger is a giant that can shut down God's possibility for our lives. If we're not careful, our anger will burn somebody else's life down. We can also count on this: unchecked anger is definitely going to burn our lives down too.

—*Goliath Must Fall*, page 144

Worship: Celebrate Your Adoption

It's hard to forgive someone for taking something from you that you need to survive. The good news is that everything you truly need to have a flourishing life is guaranteed to you through Jesus Christ. You have been adopted as a son or daughter of God, and all the unsearchable riches of his grace are yours. No matter what the people who hurt you did to you, you're more than okay. You still hurt, but you're alive and well because you belong to God.

Take some time to celebrate that so that it sinks in. Right now you may feel like what was stolen from you is of much more value than what God has given. As long as you feel that way deep down, forgiveness will be difficult. So put some energy into reversing that belief by celebrating what God has done for you.

Here's a passage to bask in:

For those who are led by the Spirit of God are the children of God. The Spirit you received does not make you slaves, so that you live in fear again; rather, the Spirit you received brought about your adoption to sonship. And by him we cry, "*Abba*, Father." The Spirit himself testifies with our spirit that we are God's children. Now if we are children, then we are heirs—heirs of God and co-heirs with Christ, if indeed we share in his sufferings in order that we may also share in his glory. I consider that our present sufferings are not worth comparing with the glory that will be revealed in us. (Romans 8:14–18)

Read this passage aloud to yourself a couple of times. Then choose a phrase or sentence that especially speaks to you. Maybe it's the part about being heirs of God and co-heirs with Christ. Maybe it's that your present sufferings aren't worth comparing with the glory that will be revealed in you. Maybe it's just that phrase, "*Abba*, Father."

Zero in on this phrase or sentence and read it aloud to yourself. If you're alone and won't be overheard, read it loudly. Exult in it. However you've been hurt, it doesn't compare with God's great love for you and how that love can change you if you let it. Pray your chosen phrase or sentence back to God in worship.

Abba, Father, I worship you because _____
_____.
You are _____
and what you have done for me is _____
_____.

After ten minutes with this passage, go back to your list of things that you're angry about. In light of what God has done for you, can you find it in your heart to forgive, and let go of some of that anger? Not stuff it back down inside you. Not minimize it, like it didn't really hurt you. But acknowledge the hurt and say you choose to not make the other person pay. It's in God's hands. He will give you justice in his time.

In the meantime, remember that you are his adopted son or daughter.

Jot down a few sentences about this worship experience to share with your group next week.

One of the positive examples given to us in the story of David and Goliath is that David didn't let the anger of Eliab slow him down. David went on and killed Goliath. David freed his people, and he took the oppressive yoke off his brothers and all the nation of Israel. David continued forward in the power of God's name and did what God called him to do. Eliab could have done that too. He wasn't going to be king, but he could have been a lot more than he was. Eliab could have been David's champion from the start.
—*Goliath Must Fall*, page 151

Proclaim: Tell Someone About Forgiveness

If you've chosen to forgive someone, or if you're getting to the place of being able to forgive someone, tell a friend. Tell them what that's like for you. Ask your friend to pray for you in this process. Telling someone will make the decision more real for you. Remember that the goal here is to set you free from the prison of bitterness.

Write a few notes about this experience to share with the group next week.

We have to get our eyes off [what others have done] and back on Jesus. We have to realize that we are held by nail-pierced hands. We have to agree that we are treasured and loved. This affirms that we believe what God did for us is greater than what anyone could do against us. This puts us back together again. This frees us to actually live our lives, to run our race, to bloom and blossom into what God says we can be. To be loved, to let go, to let God extinguish the fire that's threatening to burn our dreams to the ground.

—*Goliath Must Fall*, pages 165–166

Addiction Must Fall

If you think you are standing firm, be careful that you don't fall! No temptation has overtaken you except what is common to mankind. And God is faithful; he will not let you be tempted beyond what you can bear. But when you are tempted, he will also provide a way out so that you can endure it.

1 CORINTHIANS 10:12-13

Orientation

According to a 2016 poll:

- Seventy-eight percent of teens check their phones at least hourly. Sixty-nine percent of parents do so.

- Seventy-two percent of teens feel they must respond immediately to texts and social networking messages. Forty-eight percent of parents do so.

- Teens and parents admit to sleeping with their phones, using them during meals while others are present with them, and feeling anxiety when they are separated from their phones. More than half of the parents surveyed confessed to checking their phones while driving and said they very often or occasionally try to spend less time on their phones.

Fundamentally, half of the teens surveyed said they are addicted to their phones, and more than a quarter of parents admitted to addiction. To phones.[1]

We can get addicted to anything that promises our brains the rewards they crave. "Scientists have shown our brains get a hit of dopamine—the chemical linked to happiness—when we hear our phones beep or ring."[2] That little sound says we matter to someone. We are wanted. Needed.

That brain reward process works the same way when we're addicted to nicotine, alcohol, shopping, overeating, porn, or simply the approval of others. We can become addicted to anything we feel we can't do without, anything we turn to when life is chaotic or in a slump. In this session, we will examine the root causes of addiction and what it takes to get free from it.

We'll explore how feelings of vulnerability lead to addiction and how getting the problem out into the light can help us say good-bye to an addiction that has dogged us for years. We don't need to be controlled by our phones or anything else. That giant is dead.

Welcome and Checking In

Go around the group and invite everyone to answer one of the following questions:

- *When you think of the word* addiction, *what comes to mind?*

or

- *Why is it so easy to get addicted to things like constantly checking your phone or watching social media for likes on your Facebook post?*

Last week you were invited to participate in the "Between Sessions" section of the study.

- Did you do one of the activities? If so, which one? If not, why not?

- What are some of the things that you wrote down in reflection?

- What did you learn by engaging in these activities?

Hearing the Word

Read aloud in the group the following passage from 1 Samuel 17:38–50. As before, listen for any fresh insights as the conclusion of the David and Goliath story is read.

[38] Then Saul dressed David in his own tunic. He put a coat of armor on him and a bronze helmet on his head. [39] David fastened on his sword over the tunic and tried walking around, because he was not used to them.

"I cannot go in these," he said to Saul, "because I am not used to them." So he took them off. [40] Then he took his staff in his hand, chose five smooth stones from the stream, put them in the pouch of his shepherd's bag and, with his sling in his hand, approached the Philistine.

[41] Meanwhile, the Philistine, with his shield bearer in front of him, kept coming closer to David. [42] He looked David over and saw that he was little more than a boy, glowing with health and handsome, and he despised him. [43] He said to David, "Am I a dog, that you come at me with sticks?" And the Philistine cursed David by his gods. [44] "Come here," he said, "and I'll give your flesh to the birds and the wild animals!"

[45] David said to the Philistine, "You come against me with sword and spear and javelin, but I come against you in the name of the LORD Almighty, the God of the armies of Israel, whom you have defied. [46] This day the LORD will deliver you into my hands, and I'll strike you down and cut off your head. This very day I will give the carcasses of the Philistine army to the birds and the wild animals, and the whole world will know that there is a God in Israel. [47] All those gathered here will know that it is not by sword or spear that the LORD saves; for the battle is the LORD's, and he will give all of you into our hands."

[48] As the Philistine moved closer to attack him, David ran quickly toward the battle line to meet him. [49] Reaching into his bag and taking out a stone, he slung it and struck the Philistine on the forehead. The stone sank into his forehead, and he fell facedown on the ground.

[50] So David triumphed over the Philistine with a sling and a stone; without a sword in his hand he struck down the Philistine and killed him.

In groups of two or three, share your answers to the following questions:

What was one thing that stood out to you from the Scripture, and why?

How did David respond when King Saul tried to give him armor? Why did David choose to go into battle without the king's equipment or weapons?

Watch the Video

Play the video segment for session six. Use the following outline to record any thoughts or concepts that stand out to you.

Notes

The giant of addiction has the power to wreck our lives. It runs through the neighborhoods of our world and snuffs out dreams.

Jesus has done what was necessary to take down this giant. If addiction is part of our life, we have to believe that we can take a step today toward freedom.

We are all addicted to *something*. All of us have a need to not feel exposed—to cover up our weakness. This leads to addiction, which can be a short-term cover for an exposed heart.

When we experience rejection, or are overwhelmed, or even just bored with life, we look for ways to numb the pain. Like Adam and Eve in the Garden of Even, we retreat from the light into the shadows and try to find something to cover us up.

After Saul agreed to let David fight the giant, he tried to cover David in armor. In a way, he was saying that David needed to cover up his reality (that he was young and inexperienced), and that God wasn't extraordinary enough to do the job through him.

The enemy will try to convince you cover up and put on armor to hide the real you. But the real you is the only one whom God can use for his glory.

The key is for us to be vulnerable and choose the path toward Christ. When we are honest with God about where we are, we realize that God's grace is sufficient for us in our weakness.

Our giants don't come down in the dark but in the light. Freedom comes when we run in packs, shoulder to shoulder with people who know our true selves and can champion with us.

Group Discussion

Take a few minutes with your group members to discuss what you just watched and explore these concepts in Scripture.

1. How could a person know if he or she is addicted to the approval of other people, as opposed to just liking people's approval?

2. The cause of addiction is *pain*. How should we deal with pain instead of numbing it with an addiction? Why is it so attractive to deal with it through an addiction instead?

3. What are some of the situations that tempt you to put on false armor to protect your vulnerability?

4. When we're feeling weak, we need to go to Jesus with our weakness. Why is that hard for so many of us to do?

5. Why is it essential to tell trusted individuals about our addiction and get their support in breaking free?

6. How would you know if someone was a safe person to confide in about an addiction? What are the character qualities of a safe person?

Living from Victory

For this activity, each participant will need a small smooth stone—of a size easily grasped in one's palm—and a permanent marker (the leader can bring along a few to share).

Throughout the six weeks of this study, we have examined giants that can torment and demoralize us and keep us from victory in Christ. This week we discussed addictions; we've also discussed anger, rejection, and fear, and that subtle giant comfort.

In keeping with the story of David and Goliath, take a smooth stone—David's weapon of victory—and with a marker write on one side the words "Goliath Must Fall." On the other side, write the giant you most struggle with these days and desire to bring down. (You may choose to add this at a later time.)

Keep the stone in a visible place as an ongoing reminder of your commitment, and more importantly God's power, to defeat this Goliath in your life so you can give God the glory.

Closing Prayer

End the meeting by inviting everyone to pray silently for the person on his or her left. Pray that this person will be able to run to Jesus with any area of addiction and experience victory in his or her life. Finally, say together this prayer based on Ephesians 6:10–18:

Lord, we want to be strong in your power, not in our own efforts. Help us today to put on your armor so that we can stand against the devil's schemes. We know that we do not battle against other people but against the spiritual forces in this world. We commit each day to be equipped with the belt of truth, the breastplate of righteousness, and the readiness that comes from the gospel of peace. In addition to this, we also commit to take up the shield of faith in order to extinguish the enemy's arrows, the helmet of salvation, and the sword of the Spirit. And we commit to pray for all our fellow believers. Amen.

Session Six

You are invited to further explore the material you've covered this week in *Goliath Must Fall* by engaging in any or all of the following activities in the coming days.

Act: Examine Your Life

The first step in dealing with an addiction is admitting to yourself that you've lost control over it. It has control over you. Maybe you feel like your favorite stress-reliever is harmless and it isn't interfering with the rest of your life. Maybe you're right. But maybe you're blind to the harm because you depend on this thing or activity to feel okay.

So get a sheet of paper and write about the last time you indulged in your stress-reliever:

- Where did it take you?
- How much time did you spend? How much money?
- How did you feel beforehand and afterward?
- How does it affect key relationships in your life?
- How do you feel about it now?

- What would you like to do differently next time?
- Do you have the power in yourself to do it differently?
- If you don't want to do this exercise, why not? Is there anything that you might be avoiding?

Mention the word *addicted* and the tone in a room instantly changes. Our minds connect the word to the "big" addictions only, such as alcoholism, drug abuse, or porn. We think of addicts only as the poor souls who go to rehab. But this generation is addicted to all manner of things. Some stuff little, some stuff big. We always need to have something going on. We've always got to be filling our minds with something to distract and entertain us. A family of five can't spend an hour at the dinner table without the eyes of each person being glued to a different screen. And entertainment is certainly not the only addiction we struggle with today.
—*Goliath Must Fall*, page 168

Worship: Exalt the Real God

An idol is anything other than God that we treat as absolutely necessary to our well-being. Addiction is essentially idolatry. "A counterfeit god is anything so central and essential to your life that, should you lose it, your life would feel hardly worth living."[3] One of the ways to dethrone an idol in your life is to worship the real God.

You can worship God today in numerous ways. One way is to sing to him. Choose a recent song or an old hymn that speaks to your soul about God's greatness. Go to a private place and sing this song aloud to God. If you need to go where no one will hear you, try your car. As you sing, ask God to tell you if your favorite stress-reliever is an idol. Ask him to convict your heart with the truth.

If you're not a singer, read aloud this passage from Isaiah 40:

> [18] With whom, then, will you compare God?
>   To what image will you liken him?
> [19] As for an idol, a metalworker casts it,
>   and a goldsmith overlays it with gold
>   and fashions silver chains for it.
> [20] A person too poor to present such an offering
>   selects wood that will not rot;
> they look for a skilled worker
>   to set up an idol that will not topple.
> [21] Do you not know?
>   Have you not heard?
> Has it not been told you from the beginning?
>   Have you not understood since the earth was founded?
> [22] He sits enthroned above the circle of the earth,
>   and its people are like grasshoppers.
> He stretches out the heavens like a canopy,
>   and spreads them out like a tent to live in.
> [23] He brings princes to naught
>   and reduces the rulers of this world to nothing.
>   (Isaiah 40:18–23)

Ask yourself, "How is God greater than my addiction? How is he bigger and more powerful? How is he more reliable? How is he more ultimately real? How is he more true, good, and beautiful?" Tell him out loud how he is greater. Spend some time worshiping him for being greater than any idol.

Underneath any addiction (and our foundational need for approval) is a larger question. It's this: What problem is occurring in my life that I need to mask the pain or emptiness with an addiction? See, the drugs or the alcohol or the sex or the porn or the people or the social media or the retail therapy is only a symptom. The cause is something else. The cause lies under the surface. The root cause of most addictions is pain. The cause is sin. Somebody has rejected us. Somebody has inflicted pain on us—emotional pain, physical pain, relational pain, economic pain. This person has made us feel like we're not good enough. We're convinced we don't have what it takes. A sense of inadequacy has been branded on our lives. Our security and sense of significance have been ripped away. Our world was turned upside down, and nothing makes sense or looks clear or feels right. We are lonely or angry or tired or annoyed or frustrated or fearful or betrayed or lost or disgusted or grieving or knocked off kilter. That's the cause. The symptom is whatever addiction shows up and promises to make us feel better.

—*Goliath Must Fall*, pages 175–176

Proclaim: Discuss with a Friend

Sometime this week, go out to coffee with a friend or another group member and talk about our culture's version of freedom versus the biblical promise of freedom in Christ. Some items you can discuss include:

- What's the difference between being free to do anything we want and being free to refrain from those things that can enslave us?
- What are some of the benefits of living a free-in-Christ lifestyle?
- What keeps us from living such a lifestyle all the time?

Share some examples—both from Scripture and your lives. And consider whether you might want to hold yourselves accountable to each other about making choices that lead to freedom. Be open and truthful with each other as you share.

If there's something that is choking the breath out of our lives, then God wants that stronghold broken. That is what deliverance is all about. Yet deliverance is about more than our freedom. God alone does the work to free us, but in setting us free the aim is that much glory is given to God. . . . Jesus wants to take down our giants so we can walk free and have the life that he wants us to live. And he wants to do that so his name can be exalted above every other name in our world. That's the reason that surpasses all other reasons. It's so people around us look at our lives and say, "Your God is truly God." Our freedom and God's glory are inextricably woven together.
—*Goliath Must Fall*, pages 226–227

Use the space below to write any key points or questions you want to share with a group member sometime soon.

Notes

1. Kelly Wallace, "Half of Teens Think They're Addicted to their Smartphones," CNN, July 29, 2016, http://www.cnn.com/2016/05/03/health/teens-cell-phone-addiction-parents/.
2. Deborah Hersman, "A Potentially Deadly Addiction," *The Huffington Post*, June 28, 2015, http://www.huffingtonpost.com/deborah-hersman/cell-phones-a-potentially_b_7161074.html
3. Timothy J. Keller, *Counterfeit Gods: The Empty Promises of Money, Sex, and Power, and the Only Hope That Matters* (New York: Penguin, 2009), xviii.

Additional Resources for Group Leaders

If you are reading this, then you have probably agreed to lead a *Goliath Must Fall* group study. Thank you! What you have chosen to do is important, and much good fruit can come from studies like this one. Thanks again for sharing your time and talent.

Goliath Must Fall is a six-session study built around video content and small-group interaction. That's where you come in. As the group leader, you are invited to see yourself as the host of a dinner party. Your job is to take care of your guests by managing all the behind-the-scenes details so that when everyone finally arrives, they can just enjoy each other.

As group leader, your role is not to answer all the questions or re-teach the content—the video, book, and study guide will do most of that work. Your job is to guide the experience and cultivate your small group into a kind of teaching community. This will make it a place to process, question, and reflect, not receive more instruction.

As such, make sure everyone in the group gets a copy of the study guide. Group members should feel free to write in their guide and bring it with them every week. This will keep everyone on the same page and help the process run more smoothly. If this is not possible, see if anyone from the group is willing to donate an extra copy or two for sharing. Giving everyone access to all the material will position this study to be as rewarding an experience as possible.

Hospitality

As group leader, you'll want to create an environment conducive to sharing and learning. A church sanctuary or formal classroom may not be ideal for this kind of meeting because they can feel formal and less intimate. Wherever you choose, make sure there is enough comfortable seating for everyone and, if possible, arrange the seats in a semicircle so everyone can see the video easily. This will make transition between the video and group conversation more efficient and natural.

Also, try to get to the meeting site early so you can greet participants as they arrive. Simple refreshments create a welcoming atmosphere and can be a wonderful addition to a group study evening. If you do serve food, try to take into account any food allergies or dietary restrictions your group may have. If you meet in a home, you will want to find out if the house has pets (in case there are any allergies) and even consider offering childcare to couples with children who want to attend. Finally, be sure your media technology is working properly. Managing these details up front will make the rest of your group experience flow effectively and provide a welcoming space in which to engage the content of *Goliath Must Fall*.

Leading Your Group

Once everyone has arrived, it will be time to begin the group. If you are new to small-group leading, what follows are some simple tips to make your group time healthy, enjoyable, and effective. First, consider beginning the meeting with a word of prayer, and remind the group members to silence and put away their mobile phones. This is a way to say "yes" to being present to each other and to God.

Next, invite someone to read aloud the session's "Orientation" section from the study guide. This will get everyone interacting and on the same page regarding the week's content.

Then allow about one minute per person for the "Welcome and Checking In" time. You'll need less time in session one, but after that people will probably need a full minute to share their insights from the between-sessions activities (see below). Usually you won't answer the discussion questions yourself, but you should go first with the icebreaker question, answering briefly and with a reasonable amount of self-disclosure.

After the "Welcome and Checking In" time, your group will engage in a simple Bible study, drawn from the content of the video, called "Hearing the Word." You do not need to be a biblical scholar to lead this effectively. Your role is only to open up conversation by using the instructions provided and inviting the group into the text.

Now that the group is fully engaged, it is time to watch the video. The content of each session in *Goliath Must Fall* is inspiring and challenging, so there is built-in time for personal reflection before anyone is asked to respond. Don't skip over this part. Internal processors will need the more intimate space to sort through their thoughts and questions, and it will make the group discussion time more fruitful.

During the group discussion, encourage everyone in the group to participate, but make sure that if anyone does not want to share (especially as the questions become more personal), that individual knows he or she does not have to do so. As the discussion progresses, follow up with comments such as, "Tell me more about that" or "Why did you answer the way you did?" This will allow participants to deepen their reflections and will invite meaningful sharing in a nonthreatening way.

Note that you have been given multiple questions to use in each session, and you do not have to use them all or follow them in order. Feel free to pick and choose questions based on either the needs of your group or how the conversation is flowing. Also, don't be afraid of silence. Offering a question and allowing up to thirty seconds of silence is okay. It allows people space to think about how they want to respond and also gives them time to do so.

As group leader, you are the boundary keeper for your group. Do not let anyone (yourself included) dominate the group time. Keep an eye out for group members who might be tempted to "attack" folks they disagree with or try to "fix" those having struggles. These kinds of behaviors can derail a group's momentum, so they need to be shut down. Model active listening and encourage everyone in your group to do the same. This will make your group time a safe space and foster the kind of community that God can use to change people.

The group discussion time leads to the final and most dynamic part of this study, "Living from Victory." During this section, the participants will be invited to transform what they have learned into practical action. However, for this to be successful it will require some preparation on your part. Take time to read over each session's "Living from Victory" segment, as several of them require special materials. Reading ahead will allow you to ask group members to bring any items you might need but don't have, and will give you a sense of how to lead your group through these experiences.

Use the supply list below to make sure you have what you need for each session.

Supply List

Session One:
- One blank sheet of paper for each group member
- One pen for each group member

Session Two:
- One blank sheet of paper for each group member
- One pen or pencil for each group member
- One cross for the whole group

Session Three:
- Two blank name tags for each group member
- One blue or black marker for each group member

Session Four:
- Something the group leader can write on that the whole group can see, such as a flip chart, whiteboard, or a piece of butcher paper taped to the wall
- A marker

Session Five:
- At least one backpack fully loaded with heavy items such as books, rocks, or bottles of water. If you have a large group, you may want more than one backpack. Consider having a heavier backpack for the men and a lighter-but-still-challenging backpack for the women.

Session Six:
- Small smooth stone for each group member
- Permanent markers

Finally, even though there are instructions for how to conclude each session, please feel free to strike out on your own. Just make sure you do something intentional to mark the end of the meeting. It may also be helpful to take time before or after the closing prayer to go over that week's Between-Sessions activities. This will allow people to consider what they would like to try or ask any questions they have so everyone can depart in confidence.

Debriefing the Between-Sessions Activities

Each week, there is inter-session work where everyone is invited to choose one or more of these activities: Act, Worship, and Proclaim. Your job at the beginning of the current week's session is to help the group members debrief the previous week's experience. This time is called "Welcome and Checking In."

Debriefing something like this is a bit different than responding to questions based on the video because the content comes from the participants' real lives. The basic experiences that you want the group to reflect on are:

- *What was the best thing about the activity?*
- *What was the hardest thing?*
- *What did I learn about myself?*
- *What did I learn about God?*

There are specific debriefing questions written to help the group members process what they have learned; however, the aforementioned areas are what the "Checking In" time is designed to explore. Feel free to direct it accordingly.

Thank you again for taking the time to lead your group. May God reward your efforts and dedication and make your time together in *Goliath Must Fall* fruitful for his kingdom.

About Louie Giglio

Louie Giglio is pastor of Passion City Church and founder of the Passion movement, which exists to call a generation to leverage their lives for the fame of Jesus.

Since 1997, Passion has gathered collegiate-aged young people in events across the United States and around the world. Most recently, Passion 2017 gathered more than 55,000 students in Atlanta's Georgia Dome in one of the largest collegiate gatherings in its history.

In addition to the collegiate gatherings of Passion Conferences, Louie and his wife, Shelley, lead the teams at Passion City Church, sixstepsrecords, and the Passion Global Institute.

Louie is the author of *The Comeback, The Air I Breathe, I Am Not But I Know I Am*, and *Goliath Must Fall*. As a communicator, Louie speaks at events throughout the United States and across the globe. He is widely known for messages such as "Indescribable" and "How Great Is Our God."

An Atlanta native and graduate of Georgia State University, Louie has done post-graduate work at Baylor University and holds a Master's Degree from Southwestern Baptist Theological Seminary. Louie and Shelley make their home in Atlanta, Georgia.

Fear.
Rejection
Addiction
Anger
Comfort
... *Must* Fall

Goliath
Must
Fall

Winning the Battle Against Your Giants.

Louie Giglio

In Goliath Must Fall, Louie Giglio puts a new and empowering twist on the classic story of David versus Goliath to show how Jesus has defeated "giants" in your life such as fear, anger, and addiction that seek to hold you captive. He shows that the key to defeating these giants is to focus on the size of our God, not the height of your foes. And as these giants go down, you gain the freedom to walk confidently in the reality of Christ's victory over the enemies that seek to rob you of God's best for your life.

Louie walks us toward the road to redemption through godly wisdom and relatable transparency. He doesn't just help us conquer the Goliath's in our life; he shares his own. This book offers freedom for anyone who is willing to face their giants.

—LECRAE, GRAMMY-AWARD WINNING ARTIST,
SONGWRITER, AND PRODUCER

W PUBLISHING GROUP

AN IMPRINT OF THOMAS NELSON

passionpublishing

EVERYBODY NEEDS A
COMEBACK

We all know what it feels like when life disappoints us, or to long for something different, something better, something more. In this six-session study, pastor Louie Giglio draws on examples of people from Scripture to show how God is in the business of giving fresh starts. It will offer you encouragement and perspective if you are feeling frustrated or confused, are enduring hardship or pain, have made mistakes or are grieving, or are disappointed and feel you've lost your way.

AVAILABLE IN STORES AND ONLINE!

ARE YOU ABLE
TO RELATE?

FROM THE TIME WE ARE BORN, RELATIONSHIPS SHAPE WHO WE are and how we engage with the world. We develop a view of God and others that impacts how we relate to our family and friends. All of us desire more meaningful relationships, but where do we start? In this study, Louie Giglio explores what makes us relatable. Because God has gone to extraordinary lengths to relate to us, we can build incredible relationships with one another and ever see restoration in broken relationships that seem impossible to repair.

THOMAS NELSON
Since 1798

There is no B.C.

Before Jesus walked on water, he walked in the Garden.
Before Jesus chose his disciples, he chose Abraham.

The birth of Jesus in Bethlehem isn't the beginning of the story of Jesus. The entire Bible points to him. Filled with relevant notes, articles, essays, and book introductions, The Jesus Bible will help you follow the thread of Jesus from cover to cover. Discover a new depth to the Bible's meaning as you see him in every chapter of the story.

─────── *From the Passion Movement, with featured contributions from* ───────

LOUIE GIGLIO · MAX LUCADO · JOHN PIPER · RAVI ZACHARIAS · RANDY ALCORN